DID GOD DO THIS TO ME?

And other important questions.

by

Barry Bennett

Published by Charis Bible College
850 Elkton Dr.
Colorado Springs, CO 80907
www.charisbiblecollege.org

DID GOD DO THIS TO ME?

If God is love, how can He permit such tragedy in the world? Is He judging us for sin?

These questions and many others fill the minds of both Christians and non-Christians. How can we understand the nature of God as it relates to the realities of suffering we see in the world?

My desire to answer questions was born out of watching well known Christian leaders on TV as they were interviewed about tragedies and disasters. To my amazement, they could not explain "why God allowed bad things to happen." The opportunity to reach millions of people with the revelation of God's character, nature and love was lost. The usual 'answers' that I heard would always include the well-worn phrase, "God has everything under control."

Without realizing it, these leaders were blaming God for the suffering of millions around the world. If a self-destructing world is an example of God's "control," then why should we expect the lost to believe in this Christian God?

Learning to answer these kinds of questions and many others became the focus of my teaching ministry.

People have questions, and frequently these questions are left unanswered in our churches and ministries.

During my first 3 years of employment at Andrew Wommack Ministries, I was given the opportunity to answer questions that were sent in from around the world in response to Andrew's TV and radio broadcasts. As time went by I realized that most people have the same basic questions.

When I began teaching at Charis Bible College, I was given the opportunity to develop some new courses. I immediately decided to create a course entitled *Answers to Important Questions*. *Answers to Important Questions* is now a 2nd year course that is taught during 2 terms. Some of the questions covered in the course are included in this booklet. These questions are some of the most frequently asked.

My answers may not be satisfactory for all, and in some cases can be considered as suggestions to ponder. More could certainly be written about each topic, but my hope is that the information contained within will be helpful to the reader. God has answers to our questions and the more we get to know Him, the more His Truth will dispel our doubts and our faith in our loving Father will grow.

Barry Bennett

CONTENTS

FOREWORD

Barry Bennett is a gifted teacher and also serves as the Dean of Students at Charis Bible College Colorado. You may think I am trying to promote a book as you read the following statement/foreword, and admittedly that is true. I do say with complete honesty that he is one of the favorite teachers among our staff, faculty and guest speakers. This is not to be taken lightly because I believe some of the most gifted teachers in the world visit Charis Bible College. I have asked myself what makes him such a "hit" with the students. I believe it is a combination of his intense hunger to study the Word and know the Truth, mixed with many, many years of ministry experience.

In addition to being a "seasoned" minister, one of the things I admire about Barry is his commitment to family. He is a devoted husband, father and grandfather and is a great example to the body of Christ. Besides having his earthly family, he has many spiritual children who look to him for guidance and interpretation of the Word.

Many teachers in the body of Christ are careful to "live what they preach." While this is appreciated and admirable, I think a more excellent way is to "preach what you live." It is more passionate and reveals conviction. This is Barry.

I pray this book is a blessing to you and answers some questions that you have pondered in your heart.

May this simply be a tool that the Holy Spirit uses as a guide for further revelation of His vast love for you.

Sincerely,

Gary J. Luecke
Director
Charis Bible College Colorado

WHY DID GOD CREATE MAN KNOWING HE WOULD SIN?

God's purpose is to have fellowship with like beings, created in His image, who love and serve Him from their own desire and free will. His original vision was to fill the earth with sons of God and to extend the Garden of Eden over the face of the earth.

Such a free will being needed choices in order to truly be free, so God placed an option—the Tree of the Knowledge of Good and Evil—in the Garden giving man the freedom to choose.

God also knew that man would make the wrong choice and choose independence. God could either give up on His desire for sons and daughters created in His image who loved Him by choice or He could proceed with a plan that would provide redemption for man after he failed and give him the opportunity to return to God of his own free will.

Had God decided to not make man in His image, He would have been limited in His fellowship to angels, which do not bear His image, and His desire to fill the earth with sons and daughters would have been extinguished.

Therefore, having faith that many would indeed come to Him and live for Him of their own choice, and that He would have a family of sons and daughters through the love He showed us in Jesus, God accepted the risk (so to speak). He continued with His plan so eventually He would have a creation that reflects His goodness, love and glory.

It is God's goodness that leads us to repentance (Romans 2:4), and it is His heart that no one perish (2 Peter 3:9). He has loved the whole world (John 3:16), has reconciled Himself to sinful man and is not imputing our sins unto us (2 Corinthians 5:19). All that remains is for man to receive His love and join Him in fellowship and eternal life (2 Corinthians 5:19-21).

Eye has not seen nor ear heard the things which God has prepared for those who love Him (1 Corinthians 2:9-10). We have all eternity to enjoy with God, Who is love, and no doubt the universe will be filled with His children, abundant life and glory.

IS GOD SOVEREIGN?
(DID GOD DO THIS TO ME?)

The subject of God's sovereignty can be confusing for some. The problem begins with the definition of the word sovereign. A dictionary definition includes the words supreme, superlative in quality, undisputed ascendancy, unlimited, enjoying autonomy, freedom from external control. In this definition there is no implication of sovereign meaning "active control over all events."

God's sovereignty means that God, not man, is responsible for creating and sustaining all things, and that God had the privilege of establishing the laws and boundaries of His creation. However, once created and established, God Himself is bound to what His Word has decreed. This is where many are confused.

Some see God as capricious and without rules of conduct. They see Him as acting according to whims, intervening when it pleases Him and ignoring situations in which He is not interested. This line of thinking unjustly accuses God and attacks His very nature of love.

To understand how God's sovereignty affects His creation, we must return to the beginning. In Genesis we see that God created all things by His Word. He established order and boundaries. All living things were given the ability to reproduce, but only after their kind. Pine trees will always produce pine trees and dogs will only produce dogs. Though God is sovereign, He will not change the order that He has established. To do so would disqualify Him as God, since His Word would not be immutable.

When God created man, He created him in His own image. Man was equipped to accomplish God's purpose in creation. Man was given dominion and authority over the earth and the responsibility to govern the earth according to the nature of the Creator. He was created with God's identity (image), endued with His authority (dominion), blessed with His ability (blessing) and commissioned with His work (purpose) to subdue the earth and be fruitful and multiply (Genesis 1:26-28).

Psalm 115:16 declares that God gave the earth to the children of men. His plan was for man to derive his life from God and to accomplish his purpose in harmony with God. However, man sinned. That sin effectively *unplugged* man from God. He lost his identity, his authority, his blessing and his purpose. God now found Himself on the outside looking in, so to speak. He had given the earth to man, and man through sin had given it to the devil (Luke 4:5-6). God is still the Lord and owner of His creation, but His *tenant* had broken the lease.

For God to now intervene in the events of the world, He would have to make agreements or covenants with men. Without going into great detail here, we can find covenants throughout the Bible which enabled God to deal with man and at times judge sin. Blood must be shed for there to be covenant, and a system of sacrifices was employed. The first such sacrifice is found in the Garden of Eden when God clothed Adam and Eve with the skins of animals. Animals had to die and their blood was shed to cover the nakedness of Adam and Eve.

Because of sin, how does God now intervene in the affairs of men? Does God actively control our lives, or does He actively permit events to perfect us? Again we will return to the beginning for some help. Man, created in the image of God, had a free will. It was necessary that man be able to choose because God did not want a creation of robots. He wanted men and women who would love Him of their own volition. For that free will to exist there had to be an option for disobedience. That option was the Tree of the Knowledge of Good and Evil.

We see that God did not intervene and stop Adam and Eve from sinning, nor did He even stop the serpent from enticing Eve. He did not because He could not. He had given the earth to man and told him to subdue it and guard it. It was up to Adam to take charge, and he failed. God did not stop Adam from failing even though He knew the horrible consequences that were being released into creation.

When Cain became jealous of his brother and slew him, God did not intervene. This was the first murder—the first tragedy recorded since the fall. Why didn't God stop this murder? Why didn't He protect innocent and faithful Abel from a terrible death? The fact that God didn't intervene reveals much. God is limited by His Word. He is not less sovereign, but His sovereignty had decreed that the earth belonged to man. And because of sin, man was cut off from the life of God. Thus, God was bound by His Word not to intervene.

As we follow this reasoning throughout the Bible, we see God establishing covenants and exhorting men to choose life and to obey in order to be blessed. That was God's will, but man doesn't always do what God wants. So man suffers.

To redeem mankind and succeed in His purpose to have a family created in His image who loved Him of their own free will, God had to find a perfect man who could defeat sin (live a sinless life), defeat the enemy (Satan) and defeat death. No man is able. All are born with a nature separated from God and thus, subject to sin, the devil and death.

Therefore, God became a man (Jesus) and was born sinless. He was tempted in all ways yet without sin. He defeated the devil in a face-to-face confrontation. And He defeated death by rising again. This victory of redemption now opens the way for all those who believe to once again bear His image, have His authority, receive His blessing and accomplish His purpose.

The events that take place in the world and in our lives can be divided into two categories: those things that happen within our sphere of influence and those that happen outside of our sphere of influence. Our decisions affect our sphere of influence. This is the first important truth that we must understand.

All men continue to have a free will. That includes sinners. Men are free to choose, to obey or disobey and to live according to the flesh if they like. Those choices, while not the will of God, can and do affect those around them. Men can choose to lie, to steal, to kill, to drink and drive, to abuse their spouses, etc. None of these things are what God would want, nor does God need them to accomplish His purposes. They weren't needed in the beginning before sin, and they aren't needed now. Nevertheless, evil people exist and those around them suffer. All men and women have a sphere of influence that is impacted by their free will.

Secondly, we live in a world that is still under the influence of the devil. Paul declares him the god of this world (2 Corinthians 4:4), and Jesus said that he comes to steal, kill and destroy (John 10:10). John proclaimed that the entire world lies under his influence (1 John 5:19). This kingdom of darkness is not God's will either, and yet it exists. Those who receive His redemption by faith are translated out of the kingdom of darkness and into the kingdom of God (Colossians 1:13). They are enabled to live by faith and walk in abundant life if they so choose.

Thirdly, we must understand that the planet itself has been subjected to corruption (Romans 8:20). At the flood of Noah's day, the planet was shaken to its core as the depths were broken up and the continents were divided. Tremendous change took place that left the planet unstable and dramatically different from its original state. Now there are earthquakes, tornadoes, hurricanes, droughts, floods and fires that bring death and destruction to millions. These do not represent the will of God. He does not send them and He does not need them for His purposes. They bring death and destruction, not life and peace.

The free will of evil men, the rule of Satan and the instability of the planet are all things that are outside of our normal sphere of influence. These things will happen though God is not involved in causing them. Suffering and death are not God's will. He has commissioned us to go into the world and preach the gospel of His love. It makes no sense for God to be killing the very people we are to reach.

Within our sphere of influence, we do have authority. And we can have dominion. First, we have authority over our own minds. We can tear down every stronghold and thought that goes against the Word of God (2 Corinthians 10:5). We are responsible for renewing our minds (Romans 12:2) that we might know the will of God, which is good, acceptable and perfect.

We have authority over sickness and disease. We are endued with power from on high and commanded to heal the sick. We can speak to the elements of nature and rebuke them as Jesus rebuked the storm. He didn't rebuke all storms that night, just the one that was affecting Him at the time. We can do the same. We have authority to pray that God raise up laborers to send into the harvest to reach our loved ones with the Word of God.

We have the capacity to marry wisely and raise our children in the admonition of the Lord. We have Biblical principles concerning how to handle our finances and how to release the power of giving and receiving in our lives.

We have even been given authority over the enemy if he appears. We can submit ourselves to God, resist the devil and he will flee.

We cannot determine what will come our way, but we can determine how we are going to react to it. The storms of life will be different for each of us, but we are all enabled by God to overcome and walk in victory. We should not claim that our failures are really just God dealing with us. That would be unfair to God. He has equipped us with His Name, His Spirit, His Word, His armor, His New Covenant, His promises, the keys of the kingdom and the authority to bind and loose. If we fail, it is not His fault.

My people are destroyed for lack of knowledge . . . Hosea 4:6

So, does God control or allow bad things in our lives? The answer is: God has equipped us to live victoriously in this life no matter what may come our way. He is not the author of tragedy and destruction. We live in a fallen world and it is our responsibility to determine our level of victory in this world. We see this in the parable of the two men, the two houses and the two foundations (Matthew 7:24-27). The storm wasn't God's will and the destruction of one man's house (his life) wasn't God's will. God's will is that we be doers of the Word so that we might respond in faith when trials and temptations come our way. He wants to deliver us and prosper us. But that deliverance and prosperity depends on us, not God. God will intervene in our lives by means of our faith in Him.

Question 3

DID GOD PREDESTINE WHO IS SAVED AND WHO IS LOST?

And when the Gentiles heard this, they were glad, and glorified the word of the Lord: and as many as were ordained to eternal life believed. Acts 13:48

At first glance, Acts 13:48 could appear to teach that God chooses (i.e., appoints) people to be saved. However, when we understand the meaning of the word ordained and look more closely at the circumstances surrounding this statement by Paul, we come to a more accurate conclusion. For example, consider the words of John 1:12.

But as many as received him, to them gave he power to become the sons of God, even to them that believe on his name. John 1:12

. . . and Paul's own words in Romans . . .

For whosoever shall call upon the name of the Lord shall be saved. Romans 10:13

Clearly, salvation comes to those who receive Him. The Greek word for ordained in Acts 13:48 is tasso and means "to appoint, arrange, order, ordain or decree." It does not mean pre-ordain. The same word is used in Romans 13:1.

Let every soul be subject unto the higher powers. For there is no power but of God: the powers that be are ordained of God. Romans 13:1

In other words, God has established the principle of civil government. Applying the same mentality that some use to interpret Acts 13:48, Romans 13:1 would mean that God appointed Hitler to murder 6,000,000 Jews. This is hardly accurate. Civil government is ordained (appointed) of God, but not all individual governments are pre-ordained by God.

Let's look at Paul's other statements in Acts 13. At the time that Paul made this statement in verse 48, he was in Antioch in Pisidia (Acts 13:14), and was ministering in a synagogue. In this discourse Paul says the following:

Be it known unto you therefore, men and brethren, that through this man is preached unto you the forgiveness of sins: Acts 13:38

And by him all that believe are justified from all things, from which ye could not be justified by the law of Moses. Acts 13:39

The message of faith for salvation is being clearly presented to these Jews in Antioch of Pisidia. There is no hint of predestination being taught in this message.

And the next sabbath day came almost the whole city together to hear the word of God. But when the Jews saw the multitudes, they were filled with envy, and spake against those things which were spoken by Paul, contradicting and blaspheming. Acts 13:44-45

Now we see the context developing for the statement found in verse 48. Paul is meeting with resistance on the part of the unbelieving Jews. They had heard the word of the gospel and were rejecting it.

Then Paul and Barnabas waxed bold, and said, It was necessary that the word of God should first have been spoken to you: but seeing ye put it from you, and judge yourselves unworthy of everlasting life, lo, we turn to the Gentiles. Acts 13:46

Who determined the destiny of these unbelieving Jews? Were they pre-ordained to this destiny? No. They refused the message of God's grace and judged themselves unworthy of everlasting life.

Paul continues:

For so hath the Lord commanded us, saying, I have set thee to be a light of the Gentiles, that thou shouldest be for salvation unto the ends of the earth. And when the Gentiles heard this, they were glad, and glorified the word of the Lord: and as many as were ordained to eternal life believed. Acts 13:47-48

The Gentiles heard the very same message and received it with joy. They 'ordained' themselves (arranged and ordered themselves by faith) by receiving joyfully the message of the apostles. It does not say that God pre-ordained them to believe. It simply says that they were ordained to eternal life. They did not reject the gospel.

Those who believed in Acts 13:48 had their hearts arranged and in order so that they might believe. Others either rejected the gospel message or were not yet "in order in their hearts." God does not pre-ordain who will be saved, but as many as hear the word and are glad have arranged and ordered themselves by believing.

Question 4

WHAT HAS GOD PREDESTINED?

For God so loved the world, that he gave his only begotten Son, that whosoever believeth in him should not perish, but have everlasting life. John 3:16

For whom he did foreknow, he also did predestinate to be conformed to the image of his Son, that he might be the firstborn among many brethren. Romans 8:29

God foreknew who would receive Him by free will. We are not predestined to salvation or damnation. It is our destiny after we have believed that is predestined.

God's foreknowledge is not the same as predestination. The fact that God has foreknown who would choose to believe in Him does not mean that those choices were predestined. If you were standing on the top of a tall building and saw two cars approaching an intersection at a high speed at a 90 degree angle, you would foreknow that there is going to be an accident, but you had nothing to do with that accident. You could prepare for the outcome by calling 911, but the outcome of the accident is not under your control.

When most people speak of predestination, they fail to read the verses in their proper context. Let's see what is actually being said.

According as he hath chosen us in him before the foundation of the world, . . .

This is as far as the 'predestination believers' will read. But the verse continues.

. . . that we should be holy and without blame before him in love: Ephesians 1:4

This verse does not say that our salvation was predestined, but rather that those who are saved have a predestined destiny. We will be holy and without blame. In other words, all who choose to believe in Christ have a predetermined destiny. We will all be holy and blameless before Him.

Having predestinated us unto the adoption of children by Jesus Christ to himself, according to the good pleasure of his will, Ephesians 1:5

Again, what has been predestined? Our place in God's family. Those who choose to believe in Christ will be adopted as children. We won't be some other classification. We will all be children of God. That has been predetermined by God.

In whom also we have obtained an inheritance, being predestinated according to the purpose of him who worketh all things after the counsel of his own will: That we should be to the praise of his glory, who first trusted in Christ. Ephesians 1:11-12

Once more, what has been predestined is our function. Those who choose to believe in Christ will all, without exception, be to the praise of His glory. There won't be various, differing destinies for the saved.

For whom he did foreknow, he also did predestinate to be conformed to the image of his Son, that he might be the firstborn among many brethren. Romans 8:29

And again, those He foreknew would choose Him (free will) have a predestined result. We will all be conformed to the image of the Son, not some other image! That destiny has been predestined.

Paul is not going to contradict himself. In the same letter to the Romans he declares . . .

For the scripture saith, Whosoever believeth on him shall not be ashamed. For there is no difference between the Jew and the Greek: for the same Lord over all is rich unto all that call upon him. For whosoever shall call upon the name of the Lord shall be saved. How then shall they call on him in whom they have not believed? and how shall they believe in him of whom they have not heard? and how shall they hear without a preacher? And how shall they preach, except they be sent? as it is written, How beautiful are the feet of them that preach the gospel of peace, and bring glad tidings of good things! Romans 10:11-15

There is no hint of predestined salvation in these verses. Salvation is for "whosoever will." What has been predestined is the outcome of that saving faith. Those who believe in Christ have a predestined eternity.

1. We will be holy and without blame.
2. We will be adopted as children.
3. We will be to the praise of His glory.
4. We will be conformed to the image of His Son.

The choice is ours. The results of saving faith are predestined.

WHAT DOES IT MEAN TO WORSHIP GOD IN SPIRIT AND IN TRUTH?

God is a Spirit: and they that worship him must worship him in spirit and in truth. John 4:24

To worship God in Spirit refers to being born again of the Spirit. The only worship that is truly acceptable to God is that which comes from the regenerated spirit of man. Our lives (as believers) are a constant worship to Him as we love, serve, forgive and bless others. Only a born again believer is capable of worshipping God in the Spirit. Natural man is incapable of such worship.

To worship in Truth refers to Jesus who is the Truth (John. 14:6). He is the only mediator between God and man, and thus the only worship that is valid is that which recognizes Jesus as the only Truth. Those who do not accept or believe in Jesus are outside of the Truth.

To worship in Spirit and in Truth means to be a born again son or daughter of God who exalts Jesus as the only Way to the Father, as Redeemer, Savior and Lord.

Question 6

IS BEING "BORN AGAIN" A BIBLICAL CONCEPT REGARDING SALVATION?

Jesus only mentioned it once.

Jesus described salvation as being born again of the Spirit.

Jesus answered, Verily, verily, I say unto thee, except a man be born of water and of the Spirit, he cannot enter into the kingdom of God. That which is born of the flesh is flesh; and that which is born of the Spirit is spirit . . .

The wind bloweth where it listeth, and thou hearest the sound thereof, but canst not tell whence it cometh, and whither it goeth: so is every one that is born of the Spirit. John 3:5-6, 8

Though Jesus only mentions being born again in the above verses, we can find numerous other references that use the same kind of wording.

Paul spoke of this experience as a "new creation."

Therefore if any man be in Christ, he is a new creature: old things are passed away; behold, all things are become new. 2 Corinthians 5:17

The author of Hebrews speaks of babes in Christ.

For when for the time ye ought to be teachers, ye have need that one teach you again which be the first principles of the oracles of God; and are become such as have need of milk, and not of strong meat. For every one that useth milk is unskilful in the word of righteousness: for he is a babe. Hebrews 5:12-13

Peter speaks of newborn babes in Christ.

As newborn babes, desire the sincere milk of the word, that ye may grow thereby: 1 Peter 2:2

Paul also speaks of babes in Christ.

And I, brethren, could not speak unto you as unto spiritual, but as unto carnal, even as unto babes in Christ. 1 Corinthians 3:1

Paul speaks of his conversion as being born out of due time.

And last of all he was seen of me also, as of one born out of due time. 1 Corinthians 15:8

Paul, in Galatians, speaks of Isaac as the child of promise born after the Spirit.

But as then he that was born after the flesh persecuted him that was born after the Spirit, even so it is now. Galatians 4:29

John speaks of the born again experience later in his life.

If ye know that he is righteous, ye know that every one that doeth righteousness is born of him. 1 John 2:29

Whosoever is born of God doth not commit sin; for his seed remaineth in him: and he cannot sin, because he is born of God. 1 John 3:9

Beloved, let us love one another: for love is of God; and every one that loveth is born of God, and knoweth God. 1 John 4:7

Whosoever believeth that Jesus is the Christ is born of God: and every one that loveth him that begat loveth him also that is begotten of him. 1 John 5:1

For whatsoever is born of God overcometh the world: and this is the victory that overcometh the world, even our faith. 1 John 5:4

We know that whosoever is born of God sinneth not; but he that is begotten of God keepeth himself, and that wicked one toucheth him not. 1 John 5:18

And finally, Peter speaks of the same experience.

Being born again, not of corruptible seed, but of incorruptible, by the word of God, which liveth and abideth for ever. 1 Peter 1:23

So, there are numerous references to the born again experience, and thus, it is a major Christian doctrine and teaching.

Question 7

DOES WATER BAPTISM REMIT SIN?

Then Peter said unto them, Repent, and be baptized every one of you in the name of Jesus Christ for the remission of sins, and ye shall receive the gift of the Holy Ghost. Acts 2:38

In Acts 2:38, was Peter declaring that the remission of sins was by means of baptism?

To him give all the prophets witness, that through his name whosoever believeth in him shall receive remission of sins. Acts 10:43

Peter made this second statement while preaching to the first group of gentiles to hear the gospel. His declaration is that faith activates the remission of sins. This group of believers was then baptized in the Spirit before being baptized in water. Thus, faith alone was necessary for the remission of their sins.

And that repentance and remission of sins should be preached in his name among all nations, beginning at Jerusalem. Luke 24:47

Here Jesus commissioned His disciples to preach

repentance and remission of sin. It is curious that water baptism was not included in this sequence of events. Again, it is faith in His name that gives us newness of life.

> *For with the heart man believeth unto righteousness; and with the mouth confession is made unto salvation. Romans 10:10*

Thus, when Peter preached on the day of Pentecost (Acts 2), it cannot be interpreted as a doctrine of baptism for remission, but of repentance for remission with baptism as the response of faith that acknowledges and demonstrates that faith.

We believe that baptism is a necessary act of faith, but it is not the point of regeneration. We are baptized *because* we believe, not in order to believe. We are baptized *because* we are saved, not in order to be saved. We are baptized because our sins have been remitted by faith.

Baptism should be the action of faith that demonstrates the new birth. Baptism is not the new birth.

Question 8

DOES GOD CREATE EVIL?

I form the light, and create darkness: I make peace, and create evil: I the LORD do all these things. Isaiah 45:7

The key to understanding this statement and other similar statements found in the Old Testament can be found in Exodus 19:8 and Exodus 24:3, 7.

And all the people answered together, and said, All that the LORD hath spoken we will do. And Moses returned the words of the people unto the LORD. Exodus 19:8

And Moses came and told the people all the words of the LORD, and all the judgments: and all the people answered with one voice, and said, All the words which the LORD hath said will we do. Exodus 24:3

And he took the book of the covenant, and read in the audience of the people: and they said, All that the LORD hath said will we do, and be obedient. Exodus 24:7

In Exodus 19, God promised that if Israel would

obey Him, they would be to Him a peculiar treasure above all people. The people agreed to God's words. God then proceeded to give the Law to Moses with the blessings and judgments. When Moses returned from the mount and read the words of the Lord and the judgments, the people again agreed to the covenant. In Exodus 24:7, they again agreed to the covenant.

In so doing, they had authorized God to fulfill the words of His covenant with them. They were to be blessed for obedience and cursed for disobedience (Read Deuteronomy 28). Each disobedience obligated God to act accordingly. He had given His Word and the people had given their word.

From that moment on in the Old Testament, when we see the judgments of God on Israel and hear His pronouncements about "creating evil," it must always be understood within the context of the covenant that Israel had agreed to. God was "creating evil" for them through judgment. He was not revealing His attributes toward the world, or contradicting the revelation of Himself that we have in Jesus. He was simply keeping His obligation to judge Israel for their idolatry and disobedience.

Isaiah 45 describes the consequences that would come over Judah for their disobedience, and later their restoration during the government of Cyrus. The passage does not refer to God's ways or character apart from that specific context. When God says that He creates evil, it is speaking of the adversity prepared for Judah for having separated themselves from Him and His Word. It does not mean that God is the author of evil and darkness for the entire world.

" . . . shall there be evil in a city, and the LORD hath not done it?" Amos 3:6

Amos 3:6 is a similar situation. It must be understood within the context of the Law of Moses. God and Israel had made a covenant that included judgment and curses for disobedience.

The superior revelation of the New Testament reveals that God cannot be tempted with evil nor does He tempt any man. (James 1:13). James 1:17 reveals the true nature of God, that *"every good gift and every perfect gift is from above, and cometh down from the Father of lights, with whom is no variableness, neither shadow of turning."*

Those who would attribute evil to God or even attempt to call down evil from God were rebuked by Jesus.

For the Son of man is not come to destroy men's lives, but to save them. Luke 9:56

God is not the author of evil. Israel's disobedience to God released the judgment of the old covenant. Thank God that we have a better covenant established upon better promises!

DOES GOD JUDGE THE EARTH BY MEANS OF NATURAL DISASTERS?

The tragedies that happen in the earth are a result of sin and the work of the enemy who comes to steal, kill and destroy (John 10:10).

For we know that the whole creation groaneth and travaileth in pain together until now. Romans 8:22

Earthquakes, famines, hurricanes and other disasters do not represent the work of God, but rather are the results of sin and its effects in a planet that is "groaning and travailing in pain" under the "bondage of corruption" (Romans 8:21-22).

The planet has been subjected to corruption. At the flood in the days of Noah, the planet was shaken to its core as the depths were broken up and the continents were divided. Tremendous change took place that left the earth unstable and dramatically different from its original state. Now there exist earthquakes, tornadoes, hurricanes, droughts, floods and fires that bring death and destruction to millions. These do not represent the will of God. He does not send them.

Who will have all men to be saved, and to come unto the knowledge of the truth. 1 Timothy 2:4

It would make no sense for God to send us into all the world to preach the gospel (good news) to all men while at the same time He is destroying them through tragedies and disasters. Our gospel is good news, and God's mercy and grace have given us this time in which He is not imputing our sins unto us (2 Corinthians 5:19). He has reconciled Himself unto us and is pleading with us through the gospel that we be reconciled unto Him! (2 Corinthians 5:20)

The Lord is not slack concerning his promise, as some men count slackness; but is longsuffering to us-ward, not willing that any should perish, but that all should come to repentance. 2 Peter 3:9

Jesus made it clear that God is not judging the earth.

For the Father judgeth no man, but hath committed all judgment unto the Son: John 5:22

And Jesus also revealed how judgment would come.

He that rejecteth me, and receiveth not my words, hath one that judgeth him: the word that I have spoken, the same shall judge him in the last day . . . John 12:48

We will be judged by the Word of God in the "last day" (See Romans 2:5). Therefore, natural disasters are not God's judgment for sin. They are natural disasters that are a part of fallen nature.

WHAT ABOUT JOB?

The book of Job is often misunderstood as it relates to the Christian life. When reading Job we need to understand some of the fundamental differences between Job and a Christian believer.

To begin with, Job had no covenant with God. Job apparently lived before the time of Abraham and did not enjoy the kinds of promises that God had made to Abraham. For example, God had made a covenant with Abraham and that covenant included protection from his enemies (Genesis 15:1). Similarly, in Deuteronomy 28:7 we find the promises of God under the law also protected Israel from their enemies. However, Job was exposed to his enemies and they quickly took or destroyed everything he had. In our case, we have a "better covenant established on better promises" (Hebrews 8:6), and that covenant includes healing and protection!

Job also had no knowledge of the devil. He was not aware that the devil was the "god of this world" (2 Corinthians 4:4), "the prince of the power of the air" (Ephesians 2:2), the "thief" (John 10:10) and that the whole world was under his rule (1John 5:19, Luke 4:5-6). Job had very limited knowledge and assumed that his troubles came from God. He even accused God of afflicting him on various occasions

(Job 6:4). But we know so much more under the New Covenant. We know that our fight isn't with God but with "principalities and powers," and that we have been given faith to quench all the "fiery darts of the wicked one" (Ephesians 6:12-16).

We also see that Job had a very limited knowledge of God. He himself confesses his ignorance at the end of the book of Job when he says,

> *I have heard of thee by the hearing of the ear:*
> *but now mine eye seeth thee . . . wherefore I .*
> *. . repent in dust and ashes. Job 42:5-6*

A few verses earlier Job had declared,

> *I have uttered that I understood not, things . .*
> *. which I knew not." Job 42:3*

So, we are dealing with a man with limited knowledge. But under the New Covenant we have the maximum revelation of God, greater than the revelation of Abraham, greater than Moses and the Law. We have Jesus, God in the flesh. And we see the will of God revealed fully in Jesus when He went about doing good and healing all who were oppressed of the devil because God was with Him (Acts 10:38).

One of the most important differences between Job and a New Covenant believer is that the believer is a new creation, born again by the Spirit of God! Job was not born again, nor was anyone in the Bible before the resurrection of Jesus. Thus, they were limited to their sin nature and sensory knowledge. God could not relate to Old Testament saints as He can relate to us. We are His workmanship, created in Christ Jesus (Ephesians 2:10). Job was a natural man, with no covenant and limited knowledge.

Job also had no weapons with which to fight the enemy. Since he had no covenant, he was defenseless. However, we have been given the Name of Jesus, the power of the blood, the filling of the Holy Spirit, the precious promises of God, the armor of God, the gifts of the Spirit, the keys of the Kingdom, the Word of God, the power of faith that can move mountains, the Spirit of power, love and a sound mind, and we have been blessed with all blessings! We are well equipped to overcome the enemy and any sickness or destructive work that he may attempt to put on us.

Job lived in fear. Fear is the natural state of fallen man. Faith turned to fear when Adam and Eve sinned. Job worshipped in fear since he really didn't know who he was worshipping (Job 3:25). Fear is the basis for all the religions of the world. But faith is the foundation of the gospel.

Finally, Job didn't have an intercessor. The devil had access to God through man's sin. He could accuse man day and night, and thus he did with Job. However, Jesus has defeated sin, the devil and death and has sat down at the right hand of God and ever lives to make intercession for us (Hebrews 7:25). The accuser of the brethren has been cast down and Jesus is now interceding for us! Job did not have Jesus as his intercessor (Revelation 12:10).

Job was blessed by God because he was a man of integrity, but he was not protected by a covenant.

The accuser had full access to Job. It could appear that God was giving the devil permission to attack Job because of his (the devil's) provocative comments, but we see in James 1:13 that God cannot be tempted with evil nor does He tempt any man. So whatever we see happening in the book of Job between God and the devil, we know based on the revelation in James that the devil was not successfully provoking God to test Job or tempt him.

Job is not an example for our Christian experience, nor an example of the covenant we have by the blood of Jesus. Our covenant includes healing. Job said,

the Lord gives and the Lord takes away. Job 1:21

But God didn't say that. Jesus said,

The thief cometh not, but for to steal, and to kill, and to destroy: I am come that they might have life, and that they might have [it] more abundantly. John 10:10

Unfortunately, many choose to believe Job's words of ignorance instead of Jesus' words of revelation.

Job's story is not indicative of God's dealings with us under the New Covenant. They are not comparable in any way. Job lived with the most limited understanding of God. God's revelation to mankind is progressive. The most primitive revelation is found in Job. Then, more revelation is given through Abraham. We can understand more of God in His dealing with Israel under the Law. Isaiah prophetically reveals Jesus, the Redeemer. Then Jesus reveals God in flesh. And finally, Jesus reveals Himself to Paul. Thus, all true doctrine must start with Jesus, not Job.

Whatever God did or didn't do in Job's story has no bearing on our Covenant with Him. Satan is a defeated foe and we have been given authority over him. We are to resist him and he will flee. Satan no longer has access to God in order to accuse us. New Covenant believers should not compare themselves to Job.

Question 11

HOW CAN I KNOW THAT GOD LOVES ME?

Accepting God's love is a perpetual struggle for mankind. Man by nature (sinful, fallen nature) assumes a position of unworthiness and guilt. All of man's religions are built on the concept of fear, ignorance and guilt.

That is why Christianity is so unique. Rather than a fearful, guilt-ridden man reaching up to a mysterious, angry God, Jesus came down to us to show us the Father. He reconciled Himself to us, took all of our sins and their judgment on Himself and freely offers us His life!

Natural man has a hard time dealing with this. He feels he must do something to be accepted by God. But the love of God declares that He did it all for us. Love gives and Love forgives.

To see and comprehend love, you only have to look at Jesus. He is God's love manifested. He healed all who came to Him. He forgave sin, fed the multitudes, raised the dead and taught us how to live. Jesus is our picture of love. Jesus loves you, and there is no difference between Jesus and God. Jesus is God manifested in flesh.

Pray the following prayer, adapted from Ephesians 3:16-19. Pray it daily, meditate on it and believe that God will reveal His love to you.

"Father, grant me, according to the riches of your glory, to be strengthened with might by your Spirit in my inner man; That Christ may dwell in my heart by faith; that I, being rooted and grounded in love, May be able to comprehend with all saints what is the breadth, and length, and depth, and height; And to know the love of Christ, which passes knowledge, that I might be filled with all the fulness of God." Ephesians 3:16-19

As you spend time with Him, asking Him to reveal His love to you, you will begin to get a revelation that will transform your life.

And we have known and believed the love that God hath to us. God is love; and he that dwelleth in love dwelleth in God, and God in him. 1 John 4:16

Question 12

DOES THE LORD CHASTEN US?

For whom the Lord loveth he chasteneth,
and scourgeth every son whom he receiveth.
Hebrews 12:6

One of the questions we hear frequently concerns the idea of chastisement or discipline. What does this mean and how does God chastise us? Should we understand sickness, tragedy and the loss of jobs or loved ones as the work of God for our good?

The words chastise, chasten and chastisement mean to train, instruct, educate, teach and discipline. Here are some examples:

And, ye fathers, provoke not your children to
wrath: but bring them up in the nurture and
admonition of the Lord. Ephesians 6:4

Nurture is the same Greek word used for chasten and chastisement in Hebrews 12.

All scripture is given by inspiration of God,
and is profitable for doctrine, for reproof, for
correction, for instruction in righteousness: 2
Timothy 3:16

Instruction is the same word. Therefore, the biblical concept of chastening refers to the instruction, nurture and admonition of the Lord by means of His Word. While God's correction included physical punishment (curses) under the Old Covenant, His correction under the New is by means of the Word "that the man of God may be perfect, thoroughly furnished unto all good works." (2 Timothy 3:17)

Chastisement is often misunderstood because of our wrong concepts of God. When we study Hebrews Chapter 12 in its context we see that the author of Hebrews is not talking about God sending bad things our way, but rather exhorting, correcting and instructing the readers to resist temptation and not fail the grace of God (Hebrews 12:4, 14).

The chastening of the Lord is the exhortation to resist temptation and is similar to a child being disciplined by his father. When we resist temptation, it is often a struggle. The un-renewed mind wants one thing; the spirit wants another. Resisting temptation is not pleasant but will yield fruit.

But if ye be without chastisement, whereof all are partakers, then are ye bastards, and not sons. Hebrews 12:8

Again, the word 'chastisement' refers to the instruction, correction, discipline and nurturing of the Word of God. Those who do not heed the Word and do not resist temptation are not like sons. Sons endure a father's chastening; bastards do not, since they don't have a relationship with their father.

The author continues his chastening in Hebrews 12:12, with the same context we saw at the beginning of the chapter. "Wherefore lift up the hands which hang down, and the feeble knees . . ." In other words, hang in there! You can resist! You can overcome. It's not always easy to the flesh. It's like being disciplined, but it is worth it!

We need to understand that sickness and tragedy have never perfected anyone. Such things only come to steal, kill and destroy. The Lord has given us His word to perfect and chasten us.

MUST WE FORGIVE OTHERS FOR GOD TO FORGIVE US?

But if ye do not forgive, neither will your Father which is in heaven forgive your trespasses.
Mark 11:26

To understand Mark 11:26 or the "Lord's Prayer," in Matthew 6:9-15, we need to understand the context in which it was given. Jesus was speaking to His disciples while still under the Old Covenant, and He was teaching them to pray before He went to the cross, before He had ascended into heaven and poured out the Holy Spirit, and before the new birth was possible.

To the Jewish mind, forgiveness was understood to revolve around a system of sacrifices and law keeping. It had nothing to do with the condition of the heart. Jesus referred to this in Matthew, chapter 5 when he spoke about adultery vs. lust, and murder vs. hate. His point was to reveal that men were incapable of keeping the Law, and that the Law would never make one righteous. <u>The heart of man was the problem</u>. Thus, under the law forgiving others was also impossible because the heart of the offended person had not been changed.

Jesus was revealing the impossibility of keeping the law. If we can't be forgiven unless we forgive, then who can be forgiven? How do you know that you have fully forgiven all who have offended you? What if there is some lingering unforgiveness that you havent recognized or that you have chosen to ignore? Can you not be forgiven by God?

In the revelation of the gospel of the New Covenant given to Paul these things are explained. In Colossians 3:13, we find Paul revealing how we have been equipped to forgive. It basically says exactly the opposite of what Jesus taught to those under the law.

Forbearing one another, and forgiving one another, if any man have a quarrel against any: even as Christ forgave you, so also do ye. Colossians 3:13

Paul is showing that unless we have been forgiven and have experienced the transforming power of forgiveness (the new birth), we are unable to forgive others. But once we are forgiven and have become a new creation, and the love of God has been shed abroad in our hearts, we are now able to forgive others. He forgave us first!! Now we are able to truly forgive others.

Do you see the difference? Jesus was showing that there could be no forgiveness under the law unless forgiveness was given to others from the heart. It was a heart issue, and all men's hearts were corrupt. It isn't just murder that is wrong, but hate. It isn't just fornication that is wrong, but lust. The heart is the problem. And before Jesus' redemptive work on the cross there was no hope to fulfill such requirements.

Therefore, we see that without a sacrifice for our sins and without faith in that Sacrifice (Jesus), there is no hope for anyone. Only in Christ are we equipped to forgive others because He first forgave us! Under the law, you had to obey every jot and tittle, and Jesus even made it more stringent by speaking of heart issues—in order "to be saved." No man is able to do it. But under the grace of His redemption, God does it first! Then He asks us to forgive others as He has forgiven us.

Praise God that, ". . . we have redemption through his blood, the forgiveness of sins, according to the riches of his grace;" Ephesians 1:7

Before we are born again, we are incapable of forgiving others from the heart. Our heart is darkened and corrupt. But after we have been forgiven and born again, the love of God in our transformed heart is now able to forgive. Mark 11:26 states that we cannot be forgiven if we don't forgive, but the New Covenant reveals that He forgives us first, and we are now able to forgive others.

And be ye kind one to another, tenderhearted, forgiving one another, even as God for Christ's sake hath forgiven you. Ephesians 4:32

Question 14

IS IT GOD'S WILL TO HEAL?

God has revealed His will concerning healing just as He has revealed His will concerning salvation. He is not willing that any should perish and that all should come to repentance (2 Peter 3:9). God so loved the world that He gave His Son (John 3:16). All who call upon His Name shall be saved (Acts 2:21).

It is impossible to have faith if we don't know God's will. As one man of God has said, "Faith begins when God's will is known." As long as there is doubt, there is double mindedness, and we will receive nothing from the Lord (James 1:6-8).

We have no doubt that God will honor His Word concerning salvation. All who believe with their heart and confess with their mouth that Jesus is Lord and that God raised Him from the dead shall be saved (Romans 10:8-10). God does not respond to the faith of some and ignore the faith of others. He will save all who come to Him in faith.

The same is true concerning healing. The same redemption that saved us also healed us. In fact, the same Greek word *sozo* is used interchangeably in the New Testament to speak of salvation (forgiveness of sins) and physical healing.

If we want to know God's will concerning something, we need to look at Jesus, since Jesus came to do His will (Hebrews 10:7). Jesus healed all who came to Him and never once refused to heal anyone. He never told a single sick person that it was God's will that they suffered a little longer. He never made anyone sick "to teach them something." These are terrible lies that the enemy has sown in the church to keep God's children in bondage to sickness and doubt.

James makes it quite clear in James 5:14, when he asks the church, "Is any sick among you?" The question reveals that there should be no sick in our midst. The word sick is the Greek word *astheneo*, and means "to be feeble (in any sense), be diseased, impotent folk (man), (be) sick, (be, be made) weak." James goes on to give the answer if per chance there are some sick ones in the congregation. He declares that the prayer of faith will save the sick and the Lord shall raise him up!

To suggest that it may not be God's will to heal some would make Jesus' suffering on the cross of no effect. The Word declares that "by His stripes we were healed" (1Peter 2:24). Jesus bore all sickness so that we would not have to bear it, just as He bore all sin that we not have to pay the penalty. The power of sickness is sin, and if sin is defeated, then sickness has no legal right in the body of a believer. Sickness only exists because of ignorance, fear or rebellion.

God does not change. He is the Lord that heals us (Exodus 15:26), the Lord who sent His Word to heal us

(Psalm 107:20), the Lord who forgives all our sins and heals all our diseases (Psalm 103:1-3), the Lord who bore our sicknesses on the cross (Isaiah 53:4-5), the Lord who healed all who came to Him (Matthew 8:16), the Lord who went about doing good and healing all who were oppressed of the devil for God was with Him (Acts 10:38), the Lord who set the church against sickness and commanded us to go and to heal the sick (Matthew 10:8), the Lord who told us that greater works would we do (John 14:12), the Lord who gives us power to lay hands on the sick and they recover (Mark 16:18), the Lord who confirms His Word with signs following (Mark 16:20), the Lord who healed the sick in the early church through the ministries of Peter, Paul and other believers (Acts), the Lord who gives gifts of healings to the church for the church age (1 Corinthians 12:9), and the Lord who asks through James if there are any sick among us (James 5:14).

Healing is for all and is available to all through faith in God's grace.

Question 15

HOW DO I GET FAITH FOR HEALING?

God has provided healing for every person on the earth, just as He has provided forgiveness of sins and redemption.

<u>Our faith is the result of a loving, trusting relationship with God</u>. That relationship is the key to receiving all that He has given us, including healing. We often neglect our relationship with God until we are sick, and then we try to do things, even good things, to get something from God.

We need to understand that God has already provided what we need. He is not holding back. It is we who have not come into the "rest" of faith. We are still striving with our own efforts and "faith formulas" rather than simply receiving from Someone who loves us and whom we trust. Many deal with sin consciousness, depression or hopelessness because they think that God is unwilling or unable to heal them. This is simply not true.

Just as we have physical eyes, we have spiritual eyes. The eyes we choose to use will determine the results we see in life. We can choose to see things as God does, such as healing, deliverance, increase, protection, peace and joy. All of those things are spiritual realities. If we can *see* them, we can have them. Unfortunately, most of us are so busy meditating on what our physical eyes see that we never even consider what God has provided. But if we could *see* it, we would proclaim it and receive it.

While we look not at the things which are seen, but at the things which are not seen: for the things which are seen are temporal; but the things which are not seen are eternal. 2 Corinthians 4:18

Learning to be free from our senses is a result of being completely focused on God and His Word. Those who focus on the sickness, the medical terms, the doctor's reports, the medicine and the facts usually struggle with their faith. They have filled themselves with so much information that it blocks revelation knowledge. When we begin to see Jesus and not the sickness, faith is born.

We having the same spirit of faith, according as it is written, I believed, and therefore have I spoken; we also believe, and therefore speak; 2 Corinthians 4:13

We often confuse understanding with faith. Many times our minds grasp and believe long before it is truly conceived in our hearts. We know that faith is from the heart, not the head (Romans 10:10).

This should not condemn us. It's just the reality of learning to live by faith. We can have great victories of faith in some areas, and in others, we can still be struggling. If our faith is not where it needs to be to see the manifestation of a healing, then we have no problem seeking medical help. We don't assume that because we know it is God's will to heal us that it automatically means that our stubbornness is the same as faith.

Faith is "knowing that you know." When in your spirit you know you are healed, then you don't let the physical symptom get in your way. You continue on, knowing that the manifestation is coming from the Spirit world into the physical world. It is already done. But if it is more mental knowledge than spiritual revelation, you will be uncertain, frustrated and even fearful. That can only be remedied by receiving a word from God that will take you to a new dimension. You will know that true faith has been born by the peace and confidence it produces. You may be facing a mountain, but you know that you already have the victory.

Much of what we call a "faith battle'" is really a battle against unbelief. When faith is conceived, there is a knowing and an assurance that we have what we have believed for, even before the physical manifestation. Unbelief can only be conquered by eliminating distractions and focusing on Him and His Word. Many Christians are more focused on the distractions of life and spend very little time with the Lord. When trials come, they are unprepared and often full of doubt.

When faith is conceived, there is a kind of "faith declaration" that sets the criteria for the manifestation. That criteria is different for every person and every circumstance.

In the case of the woman with the issue of blood, her criteria or declaration of faith was that "if I but touch the hem of His garment, I will be made whole." She determined the moment of her healing, not Jesus.

In the case of the centurion and his servant, the centurion declared to Jesus, "I am not worthy that you should enter my house, but just say the word and my servant shall be healed."

Jesus was willing to go to his house, but the centurion's faith established a different level of faith. Jesus responded to him at this level.

Jairus told Jesus that if He would come lay His hands on his daughter, she would live. This was Jairus' decision, his point of faith and his criteria. Jesus responded to it.

We see this over and over as Jesus told those who were healed that it was their faith that healed them, and "be it unto you according to your faith." He was responding to their level of faith and their criteria of "if only." If only I can touch His garment; if only He will lay his hands on my daughter; if only He speaks the word.

When we are at the place of "if only," we are beyond the battle with unbelief, and we know that we know that we have our healing. This is not something we make up in our minds. This is a faith that is birthed in us as we hear His Word and get the revelation of our need being met. Nothing can shake that conviction.

Nothing can deter that kind of faith. That kind of faith will even open a hole in the roof of a house and lower the infirm man through the hole into the presence of Jesus.

That point of faith is different for everyone. It could be your faith that someone's prayer for you would be your moment of manifestation. It could be that in your own prayer time you receive the revelation of your healing. The manifestation might be gradual or instantaneous. But you know that you know.

1 Timothy 6:12 says to fight the good fight of faith. If living by faith was easy and the results instant, then there would be no need to fight the good fight of faith. Doubt, fear and unbelief are great adversaries to faith. They usually get stronger when the answer takes longer than we want.

That ye be not slothful, but followers of them who through faith and patience inherit the promises. Hebrews 6:12

DID GOD DO THIS TO ME?

Question 16

DOES THE DOCTRINE OF HEALING MEAN THAT WE WILL NEVER DIE?

The fact that we will all die (unless Jesus comes first) does not mean that we must all die sick. Sickness cuts life short. God has a purpose for each of us and that purpose will not be fulfilled if we die before our time due to sickness.

Death occurs when the spirit leaves the body (James 2:26). It can be sped up through sickness or one can finish their course as did Paul and Peter and know that the time of their departure is near (2 Timothy 4:6-7, 2 Peter 1:14).

As long as we are walking in our purpose, full of faith, we can remain healthy until the time of our departure arrives.

Because he hath set his love upon me, therefore will I deliver him: I will set him on high, because he hath known my name. He shall call upon me, and I will answer him: I will be with him in trouble; I will deliver him, and honour him.

With long life will I satisfy him, and shew him my salvation. Psalm 91:14-16

Question 17

WHAT IS FAITH?

Now faith is the substance of things hoped for, the evidence of things not seen. Hebrews 11:1

The capacity to believe is inherent in every man. Everyone believes something, and our words, thoughts and actions reveal our faith. Men will live by what they hear. Those who listen to the world will believe what the world believes and do what the world commends. That is their faith. Fallen man has taken the divine capacity to believe and has turned it inside out in order to believe something other than God's Word.

But when God's Word finds a place in our hearts, our faith becomes alive to its Source and begins to think, act and speak in agreement with God's revelation to man. The seed of the Word releases the Divine seed of faith in the heart of man.

The faith we have is the same that the apostles had.

Simon Peter, a servant and an apostle of Jesus Christ, to them that have obtained like precious faith with us . . . 2 Peter 1:1

We are told in Romans 12:3 for some to not think more highly of themselves than others because we have all received the same measure of faith. Some didn't get more and others less. Some did receive different giftings, but not a different amount or kind of faith.

Our faith is compared to a seed in Luke 17:6. Jesus taught a lot about the power of the seed. The kingdom of God functions according to the principle of the seed. The seed must be sown, and the result will be a harvest of like kind, and more seed! (Mark 4:26-29)

The point is that while all believers have the same measure and quality of faith, if it is not sown it will not develop. As we sow our faith by speaking and acting on the Word, that faith can develop enough to move mountains! (Mark 11:22-23)

This faith has only one source. We cannot pray for more faith, or fast for faith or worship for faith. Faith is only activated by hearing the word of God.

So then faith cometh by hearing, and hearing by the word of God. Romans 10:17

As we hear the Word of God concerning our redemption, forgiveness, healing, victory, etc., that Word contains within it the faith of God. The Word is a seed and faith is a seed. The seed of divine faith is contained in the seed of the Word.

The faith that we released to be saved is the same faith that we must release to be healed. We appropriate all of the promises of God by that same faith! We simply must hear the Word in our spirits to know what has been deposited in us. Once we know, we speak.

We having the same spirit of faith, according as it is written, I believed, and therefore have I spoken; we also believe, and therefore speak; 2 Corinthians 4:13

Faith is the result of God's revelation to man, which produces conviction, certainty and a corresponding action.

As we learn the power of the faith that is within us, and as we are made aware by the Word of all the potential of that faith, we begin to sow that measure in every area of our lives and we see the resulting harvest of blessings.

DID GOD DO THIS TO ME?

Question 18

HOW DO I PRAY FOR A LOST LOVED ONE?

The keys to praying for others can be found in the words of Jesus and Paul.

1. Pray that God would send laborers into their lives who would transmit the gospel in a way that is relevant to them. It is the Word of God that opens the hearts and transforms them.

Then saith he unto his disciples, the harvest truly is plenteous, but the labourers are few; Pray ye therefore the Lord of the harvest, that he will send forth labourers into his harvest. Matthew 9:37-38

2. Pray that the Word would reach their heart and reveal God's love. The revelation of God's love is the most important revelation that one can receive. Love this person with the love of God.

For this cause I bow my knees unto the Father of our Lord Jesus Christ, Of whom the whole family in heaven and earth is named, That he would grant you, according to the riches of his glory, to be strengthened with might by his Spirit in the inner man; That Christ may dwell in *your hearts by faith; that ye, being rooted and grounded in love, <u>May be able to comprehend with all saints what is the breadth, and length, and depth, and height; And to know the love of Christ, which passeth knowledge, that ye might be filled with all the fulness of God.</u> Ephesians 3:14-19*

3. Pray that the Spirit would convict them of their need and the gift of righteousness. This is not a condemning conviction but a revelation of their lostness and that Jesus is the answer.

And when he is come, he will reprove the world of sin, and of righteousness, and of judgment: Of sin, because they believe not on me; John 16:8-9

4. Pray that the seed of the Word that already exists in their heart, or that will be heard by them, will spring up and grow in their life. Believe that the Word of God will transform their heart and mind.

And he said, So is the kingdom of God, as if a man should cast seed into the ground; And should sleep, and rise night and day, and the seed should spring and grow up, he knoweth not how for the earth bringeth forth fruit of herself; first the blade, then the ear, after that the full corn in the ear. But when the fruit is brought forth, immediately he putteth in the sickle, because the harvest is come. Mark 4:26-29

5. Pray that they would have a revelation of

God's goodness. It is His goodness that leads us to repentance.

> *Or despisest thou the riches of his goodness and forbearance and longsuffering; not knowing that the goodness of God leadeth thee to repentance? Romans 2:4*

Question 19

WHAT IS SPIRITUAL WARFARE?

The topic of "spiritual warfare" has led to many erroneous teachings and activities that have diverted the Body of Christ away from its primary call of preaching the gospel. For some reason, many fine Christians feel that Jesus' redemptive work on the cross was not enough, and they must add to it or complete it by waging warfare against the enemy. This is simply not biblical.

All principalities and powers were spoiled by Jesus (Colossians 2:15), and He has translated us from the kingdom of darkness into His own kingdom (Colossians 1:13).

There are no more principalities to defeat and there are no more sins to atone for. Jesus has completed redemption for mankind and God has reconciled Himself to us and does not impute our sin (2 Corinthians 5:19-20). The judgment for sin was paid by Jesus (1 John 2:2). For that reason Jesus proclaimed,

All power is given unto me in heaven and in earth. Go ye therefore, and teach all nations, baptizing them in the name of the Father, and of the Son, and of the Holy Ghost: Teaching

them to observe all things whatsoever I have commanded you: and, lo, I am with you alway, even unto the end of the world. Amen. Matthew. 28:18-20

Jesus did not tell us to go attack principalities and powers, nor to ask forgiveness for the sins of our forefathers. He told us that He had all power and authority and we were to go and preach. It is so simple but we have made it complicated.

The wrestling mentioned in Ephesians 6:10-18 has nothing to do with an offensive attack against heavenly principalities. It is speaking of a defensive preparation against temptations against our flesh here on the earth. The strongholds mentioned in 2 Corinthians 10:3-5 are not demons but rather thoughts, concepts, philosophies, superstitions, political beliefs, customs, etc., that go against the Word of God. They can only be brought down by the preaching of the Word.

What is clear from the New Testament is that there is no evidence whatsoever, nor any instruction that reveals a spiritual war in high places that requires our strategic prayer and intercession. Jesus never sent forth intercessors to prepare the way for His message. He sent his disciples to preach the gospel, heal the sick and cast out demons. Jesus never indicated that some regions wouldn't receive Him because of demonic principalities, and therefore they must first be torn down before the gospel could be preached. He told his disciples to shake the dust from their feet and move to the next village if they were not received. So much for blaming demons for men's hardness of heart!

Paul never prayed to identify the strongman over a city or region. He simply preached the gospel and let the chips fall where they may. At times he was received with gladness and other times he was stoned. No mention was made of the stronghold that must be torn down. No intercessory prayer group was formed to attack these powers so that Paul could be invited back to town.

What Jesus did commission the church to do was preach the gospel.

And Jesus came and spake unto them, saying, All power is given unto me in heaven and in earth. Go ye therefore, and teach all nations, baptizing them in the name of the Father, and of the Son, and of the Holy Ghost: Teaching them to observe all things whatsoever I have commanded you: and, lo, I am with you alway, even unto the end of the world. Amen. Matthew 28:18-20

All power (authority) was given unto Jesus in heaven and in earth. In other words, there is no realm that is not subject to His authority. Therefore, we are authorized and empowered to take the gospel to all nations regardless of principalities, strongmen and strongholds. The authority of those powers has been defeated.

And having spoiled principalities and powers, he made a shew of them openly, triumphing over them in it. Colossians 2:15

These are the same principalities and powers

referred to in Ephesians 6. If Jesus has spoiled these powers, and if all authority has been given Him in heaven and in earth, and if He has commissioned us to "go into all the world and preach the gospel," then it can be assumed that the only resistance we have to deal with is an earthly resistance comprised of the strongholds in the minds of men and the fiery darts of an enemy who has been defeated and spoiled.

With the weapons of our warfare, we have been equipped for victory. Much time and prayer has been spent fighting an enemy by binding him in his heavenly abode, when in fact it is his earthly activities of lies and temptations that we have been equipped to tear down. And much time has been lost that should have been spent going into all the world and preaching. But, praying strategically sounds so much more visionary than actually preaching to the lost and healing the sick. You can stay at home and do so-called "strategic warfare," but you must leave the prayer room and go to the nations if we are to fulfill the Great Commission.

To imply that we must ask forgiveness for "the sins of the fathers" would mean that Jesus did not bring forgiveness to the entire human race through His sacrifice and His blood. Can you name one sin that was not included on the cross? Jesus was made sin! (2 Corinthians 5:21) He was made a curse! (Galatians 3:13) And God reconciled Himself to the entire world and is not imputing our sins against us (2 Corinthians 5:19).

Unfortunately, modern teaching would have us attack the heavenly powers first before feeling that we can preach the gospel with any effectiveness. This is not the New Testament pattern. There are two results from this line of thinking: 1) Men are not considered responsible for their hardness of heart; it's the devil's fault; and 2) Our lack of effectiveness in healing the sick and setting the captives free isn't our fault either. We just need to tear down some more strongholds in prayer and maybe then we can see a revival. I believe this to be an error that has sidetracked the church from its true calling and commission.

DID GOD DO THIS TO ME?

DID THE GIFTS OF THE SPIRIT PASS AWAY WITH THE APOSTLES?

Let's look at three reasons that confirm that the gifts of the Spirit remain alive in the church today.

And he said unto them, Go ye into all the world, and preach the gospel to every creature. He that believeth and is baptized shall be saved; but he that believeth not shall be damned. And these signs shall follow them that believe; In my name shall they cast out devils; they shall speak with new tongues; They shall take up serpents; and if they drink any deadly thing, it shall not hurt them; they shall lay hands on the sick, and they shall recover. Mark 16:15-18

1. In Mark 16:15-18, the command is to go into all the world and preach the gospel. Immediately we see that this command is not just for the original apostles of the Lord since it was physically impossible for them to accomplish this commission. Not only were they limited by the length of their earthly lives, they also were limited by the lack of available transportation to

reach every tribe and nation on earth.

Jesus' commission wasn't just to them, but to the entire church. If not, then we are not called to preach the gospel today because that commission died with the last apostle. This is a serious point. Are we or are we not called to reach the nations with the gospel? Was this command only to the apostles of the Lord? If the command is viable and active for us today, then what follows is also pertinent.

In Mark 16:16, *"He that believeth"* refers to those of the nations who become believers at the preaching of the gospel.

In verse 17, *"These signs shall follow them that believe,"* is a promise to those same new believers. The new believers of verse 16 are the same believers who have signs following them in verse 17.

What signs will follow these new believers? They shall cast out demons, they shall speak with new tongues, they shall take up serpents (as in the case of Paul on the island, when one attached itself to him and he suffered no harm), if they drink any deadly thing, it shall not hurt them, and they shall lay hands on the sick and they shall recover.

In verse 20, the Lord was working with them confirming the Word with signs following. The Lord is still working with those who believe and still confirms the Word with signs following.

If the preaching of the gospel is to reach all nations, then the signs that follow that preaching are still valid.

And those who respond to that preaching will also have signs follow. Logic dictates that the apostles of the Lord couldn't be around generation after generation to lay hands on each new believer. The power wasn't the apostle's, it was the Lord's power and confirmed the gospel. It still does.

2. The promise of the Father (Luke 24:49, Acts 1:4) was received by the 120 on the day of Pentecost and was preached by Peter on that same day as being for "as many as the Lord our God shall call" (Acts 2:39). This promise of power and signs is for all who call upon him.

3. For the gifts (charisma) and calling of God are without repentance "ametameletos" (irrevocable). (Romans 11:29)

These irrevocable, charis gifts are described in 1 Corinthians 12:4-11.

Now there are diversities of gifts (charisma), but the same Spirit. 1 Corinthians 12:4

So, we have the witness of three. 1)The Great Commission to all nations with signs following; 2) the Promise of the Father of the Baptism of the Holy Spirit (endued with power from on high—choose your favorite term), which is for all who come to the Lord; 3) and the gifts of God, which are irrevocable.

We can add to that Paul's clear statement in 1 Corinthians 1:7

So that ye come behind in no gift; waiting for the

coming of our Lord Jesus Christ: 1 Corinthians 1:7

Paul's understanding was that the gifts of the Spirit would be in operation until the coming of the Lord. We can confirm this with the famous quote of Jesus in Acts 1:8.

But ye shall receive power, after that the Holy Ghost is come upon you: and <u>ye shall be witnesses</u> unto me both in Jerusalem, and in all Judaea, and in Samaria, and unto the <u>uttermost part of the earth</u>. Acts 1:8

This *promise* is the power that we need to reach the nations with the gospel of God's love. Until that commission is completed, the power is here and available to those who believe.

Jesus declared: *And this gospel of the kingdom shall be preached in all the world for a witness unto all nations; <u>and then shall the end come</u> Matthew 24:14*

Once this gospel is preached to all the world as a witness (Acts 1:8), then the power, the signs, the tongues and other gifts will have fulfilled their purpose. There will be no more need. But as long as the Great Commission is in effect, the power, the gifts and the signs are *irrevocable*.

SHOULD CHRISTIANS KEEP THE SABBATH?

The Sabbath was not a 24-hour day instituted by God from creation. The Sabbath was meant to be the continual state of mankind, i.e., peace with God. Adam and Eve sinned during the Sabbath rest of God and destroyed the peace of creation. God's rest was meant to be a permanent rest. He wasn't going to go back to work the next day and rest again on the following 7th day.

Once that rest was lost, the Sabbath was constituted as a day under the Law in which fallen man was commanded to remember God and the paradise of rest that had been lost through sin. The Law of the Sabbath became a work that had to be obeyed.

Under the Law of Moses, Israel failed to enter the rest of God because of unbelief (Hebrews 4:6). As a result, since the Law could not re-establish the rest of God, there is now announced another day in which to enter God's rest. It is called Today (Hebrews 4:7).

For he spake in a certain place of the seventh day on this wise, And God did rest the seventh day from all his works. And in this place again, If they shall enter into my rest. Seeing therefore it remaineth that some must enter therein, and they to whom it was first preached entered not in because of unbelief: Again, he limiteth a certain day, saying in David, Today. . . Hebrews 4:4-7

Hebrews 4:9 declares that there remains a rest to the people of God. Obviously, if the Sabbath day under the law of Moses was adequate and met the purposes of God, there would be no discussion of another day, today, and the rest that it implies.

That rest is described as ceasing from our works, which refers to works of the Law or works of righteousness (our own) in order to please God. Those works will never attain the rest of God that is promised to His people. Keeping a day of the week can never make one acceptable and worthy of the rest of God. The rest of God was lost in Eden and can only be restored in Jesus. And what is that day of rest called? Today!

Today means that the Sabbath is not a 24-hour period, but rather a state of being. This speaks of the New Creation, of being born again, of ceasing from our works to please God and entering into His rest through Jesus Christ. Paul says:

One man esteemeth one day above another: another esteemeth every day alike. Let every man be fully persuaded in his own mind. He that regardeth the day, regardeth it unto the Lord; and he that regardeth not the day, to the Lord he doth not regard it. Romans 14:5-6

Paul referred to those who "regarded days" in Romans 14:5-6. He recognized that some born again Jews were accustomed to keeping a literal Sabbath day, and it would be hard for them to change that custom. But there were Gentile believers who had no such custom and should not be forced to keep a symbol since the symbol had been fulfilled in Christ.

So we see that it is a matter of personal conviction as to whether or not we keep a certain day unto the Lord. There is flexibility in the Kingdom to accommodate one's faith and understanding.

Let no man therefore judge you in meat, or in drink, or in respect of an holyday, or of the new moon, or of the sabbath days: Which are a shadow of things to come; Colossians 2:16

Literal Sabbath keeping is a shadow. Some may find significance in keeping a literal Sabbath, and others will not.

When the early church met for its first conference regarding doctrine, the Law of Moses was the topic. The Law, of course, includes the keeping of the Sabbath day. In Acts 15:5 we find the controversy stated, and in verse 6 we see that the apostles and elders considered the matter. Peter then speaks forth the heart of God on this matter and refers to the Law of Moses as a "yoke...which neither our fathers nor we were able to bear."(Acts 15:10)

Finally, James concludes concerning the Gentile believers, that they stay away from idols, from fornication, from eating strangled animals (not properly butchered) and from eating blood (as some cultic religions practiced). It is notable that the Gentile believers were not admonished to keep the Sabbath. This would have been God's chance to nail that down for the New Testament church, and He didn't. Why not? Because, the Sabbath was never meant to be a day of the week but rather a spiritual position of peace with God.

Therefore, the Sabbath is now not a day but represents the "new creation" in Christ! Jesus has opened the door by faith to the "rest of God" which was lost in Eden. We are no longer under a works mentality such as the keeping of laws, rituals, days and feasts. We now have the reality in the Person of Jesus Christ!

Our faith in Him is our rest and our peace with God (Romans 5:1). We are free to observe days if that is our faith or not observe them if that is our faith. Every day of the week has the same importance. Christ is our Sabbath rest, not a 24-hour day.

Question 22

WHAT ABOUT TONGUES?

Every Christian is born of the Spirit (John 3:5) and if he does not have the Spirit, he is not of God (Romans 8:9). The born again experience joins us to God, and we become one spirit with Him (1 Corinthians 6:17). This can be compared to the well of living water that Jesus spoke of in John 4:14.

But whosoever drinketh of the water that I shall give him shall never thirst; but the water that I shall give him shall be in him a well of water springing up into everlasting life. John 4:14

But, there is another experience that Jesus speaks of as *"rivers of living water"* that shall flow from within (John 7:37-38).

He that believeth on me, as the scripture hath said, out of his belly shall flow rivers of living water. John 7:38

At the moment of the new birth, the believer is baptized *by* the Spirit *into* the body of Christ.

For by one Spirit are we all baptized into one body . . . and have been all made to drink into one Spirit. 1 Corinthians 12:13

However, being baptized by the Spirit into the body—being born again, a new creation—is not the same as being baptized in or with the Spirit by Jesus. In the first case, it is the Spirit who immerses us into the body of Christ. In the second case it is Jesus who fills us or immerses us into the Spirit. These are two different events.

The immersion of the born-again believer into the Spirit can happen at any moment after being born again. It is called, the promise of the Father (Luke 24:49, Acts 1:4, Acts 2:39), being endued with power (Luke 24:29), receiving power (Acts 1:8), being baptized in or with the Holy Spirit (Acts 1:5 and many others), being filled with the Spirit (Acts 4:31), receiving the Holy Spirit (Acts 8:15-17), having the Holy Spirit fall on you (Acts 11:44) and having the Holy Spirit come upon you (Acts 19:6). This event happens subsequent to believing and being born again in every example mentioned.

Speaking in tongues, or praying in the Spirit, is the normal manifestation and is available to all who are baptized in the Spirit, though not all step out in faith and release this gift. Prophecy is another manifestation mentioned in scripture.

There are three kinds of tongues mentioned in the New Testament. The first kind we see on the day of Pentecost when every man heard the gospel in his own language. These tongues needed no interpretation. These languages were understood by those who heard them speak. The second kind we find in the church meeting when it must be interpreted and only two or three should give such a message in tongues.

The third kind involves praying in the Spirit and speaking mysteries that edify us and build us up on our most holy faith. Paul said he speaks in tongues more than all, but not in the church. So the question is, where? And then he says he wished that all spoke in tongues. This then is the prayer language that is available to all Christians who have been filled with the Holy Spirit.

When we ask for the Holy Spirit in faith, believing that we received when we ask (because God cannot lie), then we know we have it. The manifestations are different for every person. But we don't walk according to our feelings or lack of feelings. We walk by faith.

If ye then, being evil, know how to give good gifts unto your children: how much more shall your heavenly Father give the Holy Spirit to them that ask him? Luke 11:13

When we believe that the anointing and power of the Spirit have been poured out upon us, we can begin to release the gifts of the Spirit in our lives.

The heavenly prayer language exists in the believer who has asked to be filled with the Holy Spirit. It's just a matter of releasing it. As we praise God in English, we can simply switch over to a heavenly language that our mind won't comprehend.

It is similar to receiving the inspiration for a song. We hear it on the inside, but it is up to us to take paper and pen and write down the impressions that we have. God doesn't force us to write, nor is it "automatic handwriting."

So it is with speaking in tongues. The inspiration of the Spirit is within, and we provide the vocal chords, the tongue, the lips and the will. We can start and stop and speak loudly or softly as we wish. The Spirit gives the inspiration, but we control how much we want to release.

So it is with the other gifts as well. We have inspirations, ideas, burdens etc., and we begin to step out in faith with words or actions to bless others. We "know that we know" that the ability of God is within us and that He wants to flow through us. But we must get out of the boat. God does not force these things, nor take over our bodies and make us do things without our cooperation.

Question 23

WHAT ABOUT THE TITHE?

Thou shalt not muzzle the ox when he treadeth out the corn. Deuteronomy 25:4

For it is written in the law of Moses, Thou shalt not muzzle the mouth of the ox that treadeth out the corn. Doth God take care for oxen? 1 Corinthians 9:9

For the scripture saith, Thou shalt not muzzle the ox that treadeth out the corn. And, The labourer is worthy of his reward. 1Timothy 5:18

Many in the church today are attacking the concept of tithing as a relic of the Old Testament law and something that is not required under the gospel of grace.

The issue is not whether or not the New Covenant Christian is still under the law of Moses. When we approach the subject of tithing only as a feature of the law, then obviously I would agree that the Christian is not under the law nor the curse of the law if he doesn't tithe. But is that the whole story?

Many will point out that New Testament giving

should be an issue of the heart (personal desire) with no stipulations or order necessary. They point to 2 Corinthians 9:5-12 as the pattern for New Testament giving. The giving of voluntary offerings as described in 2 Corinthians 8 and 9 is certainly a dynamic part of the New Covenant lifestyle, but did you know that freewill offerings were also a feature of the law of Moses?

And thou shalt keep the feast of weeks unto the LORD thy God with a tribute of a freewill offering of thine hand, which thou shalt give unto the LORD thy God, according as the LORD thy God hath blessed thee: Deuteronomy 16:10

If freewill offerings are the new standard for the church, then we are still following the law in our giving! The whole argument of those against tithing is that we are now free from the law, but they then promote voluntary giving without realizing that such freewill offerings were also a part of the law they are trying to escape. (See Leviticus 22:18, 21, 23, Numbers 15:3, Deuteronomy 12:17; 23:23, Ezra 1:4; Ezra 3:5, Ezra 7:16; 8:28).

Is God now against freewill offerings as much as some would suggest He is against tithing? If we are going to be consistent in our approach to the subject of giving, we need to be honest and not single out tithing as "law keeping" while freewill offerings are "grace giving." Both were features of the law of Moses.

While tithing under the law was a multifaceted subject and included various tithes at different times of the year for different purposes, there is one principle that Paul emphasized that is the basis for New

Testament "tithing." This principle really has more to do with the fundamental plan of God for the extension of the Kingdom than it has to do with the ceremony and ritual of tithing under the law.

> Or I only and Barnabas, have not we power to forbear working? Who goeth a warfare any time at his own charges? who planteth a vineyard, and eateth not of the fruit thereof? or who feedeth a flock, and eateth not of the milk of the flock? Say I these things as a man? or saith not the law the same also? For it is written in the law of Moses, Thou shalt not muzzle the mouth of the ox that treadeth out the corn. Doth God take care for oxen? Or saith he it altogether for our sakes? For our sakes, no doubt, this is written: that he that ploweth should plow in hope; and that he that thresheth in hope should be partaker of his hope. If we have sown unto you spiritual things, is it a great thing if we shall reap your carnal things? If others be partakers of this power over you, are not we rather? Nevertheless we have not used this power; but suffer all things, lest we should hinder the gospel of Christ. Do ye not know that they which minister about holy things live of the things of the temple? and they which wait at the altar are partakers with the altar? Even so hath the Lord ordained that they which preach the gospel should live of the gospel. 1 Corinthians 9:6-14

For some reason this passage is overlooked and seldom considered in the subject of tithing. However, if we evaluate what Paul is saying, he is making a strong argument for the continuation of the spiritual principle of tithing with respect to fulfilling God's purpose for the sustenance of His ministers.

Apart from all of the other aspects of tithing under the law of Moses, there was one overriding principle. *"They which minister about the holy things live of the things of the temple."* What does this mean? Much of what the people of Israel brought before the Lord was for the use of the priests who ministered in the tabernacle/temple. They had no other inheritance or source of income. Their inheritance was the Lord and the Lord sustained them through the tithes, first fruits and freewill offerings that the people gave according to the law.

Paul not only appeals to this principle in his argument, he also declares that the Lord has ordained that they, which preach the gospel, should be supported in similar fashion. In other words, the support of God's ministers under the New Covenant is to follow the pattern that was established under the Old Covenant. The spiritual principle that transcends the law and continues on under the New Covenant is this: the ministers of God are to be sustained through the orderly giving of God's people.

This is not an issue of "feeling led" to give or not give. This is something that God has ordained. The term tithe while offensive to some is simply the most convenient way to describe what God expects of His people. Regardless of the term, the principle that God has established is not voluntary. It is not a freewill offering such as we find in 2 Corinthians 9. It is a spiritual principle that God's people need to fulfill.

Let's look at this in another passage that uses the same verse as its foundation.

Let the elders that rule well be counted worthy of <u>double honour</u>, especially they who labour in the word and doctrine. For the scripture saith, Thou shalt not muzzle the ox that treadeth out the corn. And, the labourer is worthy of his reward. 1Timothy 5:17-18

Again, Paul appeals to the principle of the laborer and his reward found in the law. He speaks of this principle with relation to the elders who minister in the word and doctrine. They are worthy of 'double honor.' In the Greek we find the word 'honor' means: 'a value, i.e. money paid.'

Paul is exhorting Timothy to make sure the ministers are cared for properly. Those who rule well are worthy of a "double salary" so to speak. Where does this money come from? Was Timothy to pay them from his own resources? Where did Timothy's money come from? It seems quite apparent that the churches in question had a budget. Double honor or salary would suggest a fixed amount that could be doubled. This can only mean that the church was faithfully and regularly giving to the support of the ministers. They weren't just giving as they "felt led."

I robbed other churches, taking <u>wages</u> of them, to do you service. And when I was present with you, and wanted, I was chargeable to no man: for that which was lacking to me the brethren which came from Macedonia supplied: and in all things I have kept myself from being

burdensome unto you, and so will I keep myself.
2 Corinthians 11:8-9

Paul makes a very revealing comment in this passage. While he had the apostolic authority to demand his provision from those to whom he was ministering, he chose not to use that authority (1 Corinthians 9), but rather was provided for by receiving his wages from other churches. Paul did not want to burden the new work with his needs, but others did pay his wages as God had ordained. The term robbed simply means that it wasn't the responsibility of the churches in Macedonia to support him. The salary due him should have come from the Corinthian believers, but as they were unprepared to meet that obligation, others had to step in.

We find a similar situation in Paul's letter to the Philippians.

But I rejoiced in the Lord greatly, that now at the last your care of me hath flourished again; wherein ye were also careful, but ye lacked opportunity. Not that I speak in respect of want: for I have learned, in whatsoever state I am, therewith to be content. I know both how to be abased, and I know how to abound: every where and in all things I am instructed both to be full and to be hungry, both to abound and to suffer need. I can do all things through Christ which strengtheneth me. Notwithstanding ye have well done, that ye did communicate with my affliction. Now ye Philippians know also, that in the beginning of the gospel, when I departed from Macedonia, no church communicated with *me as concerning <u>giving and receiving</u>, but ye only. For even in Thessalonica <u>ye sent once and again</u> unto my necessity. Not because I desire a gift: but I desire fruit that may abound to your account. But I have all, and abound: I am full, having received of Epaphroditus the things which were sent from you, an odour of a sweet smell, <u>a sacrifice acceptable, wellpleasing to God. But my God shall supply all your need according to his riches in glory by Christ Jesus</u>. Philippians 4:10-19*

Again we find Paul on the mission field with no support from those to whom he is ministering. But the Philippians are being commended for "once and again" supplying Paul with the means to live and carry on. In fact, Paul describes this giving as a sacrifice. In other words, this wasn't a "freewill offering" that was being given from their excess. The Philippians were doing what God had ordained. They were sacrificing for the support of God's minister. They were tithing in the New Testament concept of the principle. And Paul declared that such sacrificial giving came with a promise! First he referred to this command of God with the phrase, "giving and receiving," then mentioned that this sacrifice was "well pleasing to God," and finished by stating that God's response to this orderly giving would be to supply all of their needs!

In other words, when we do what God has ordained, He makes a promise that accumulates "fruit unto our account." We have a heavenly account that grows according to our obedience to what God has ordained: "You shall not muzzle the ox that treads the grain." This is New Testament tithing. It is not optional.

It is not freewill giving. It is the orderly giving (even sacrificial) that supplies the needs of God's ministers and ministries. It can even be budgeted so that some may receive a "double salary."

This New Testament tithing is not under a curse. You may choose to not do what God has ordained. You will not be cursed. Jesus has destroyed the curse of the law. But, doing what God has ordained does include a promise. God is "well pleased" with our giving, and He will supply the needs of those who follow this principle.

Grace will always do more than the law demands. Supporting our ministers, ministries and churches is not only something that God has ordained, it is also a key to releasing God's provision in our lives.

Question 24

WHAT ABOUT ANANIAS AND SAPPHIRA?

There are two ways to view what happened to Ananias and Sapphira. The first has to do with the gravity of the sin they committed. The second has to do with the authority of the church to deal with unrepentant sin.

1. Ananias and Sapphira lied to the Holy Spirit. This could be the blasphemy or the "sin unto death" from which there is no repentance.

> *Wherefore I say unto you, all manner of sin and blasphemy shall be forgiven unto men: <u>but the blasphemy against the Holy Ghost shall not be forgiven unto men.</u> Matthew 12:31*

> *If any man see his brother sin a sin which is not unto death, he shall ask, and he shall give him life for them that sin not unto death. <u>There is a sin unto death</u>: I do not say that he shall pray for it. 1 John 5:16*

In that light it seems possible that the lie itself was the sentence of death. They fellowshipped with the church, but were not of the church.

> *These are spots in your feasts of charity, when they feast with you, feeding themselves without fear: clouds they are without water, carried about of winds; trees whose fruit withereth, without fruit, <u>twice dead, plucked up by the roots</u>; Jude 1:12*

> *For there must be also heresies among you, that they which are approved may be made manifest among you. 1 Corinthians 11:19*

> *Wherefore whosoever shall eat this bread, and drink this cup of the Lord, unworthily, shall be guilty of the body and blood of the Lord. 1 Corinthians 11:27*

> *For he that eateth and drinketh unworthily, eateth and drinketh damnation to himself, not discerning the Lord 's body. For this cause many are weak and sickly among you, and many sleep. 1 Corinthians 11:29-30*

And again . . .

> *They profess that they know God; but in works they deny him, being abominable, and disobedient, and unto every good work reprobate. Titus 1:16*

Ananias and Sapphira were openly lying to the Holy Spirit, a sin from which there is no forgiveness. In this scenario, the lie was a sin unto death.

2. Jesus gave authority to the church for the sake of discipline and correction.

Whose soever sins ye remit, they are remitted unto them; and whose soever sins ye retain, they are retained. John 20:23

And if he shall neglect to hear them, tell it unto the church: but if he neglect to hear the church, let him be unto thee as an heathen man and a publican. Verily I say unto you, whatsoever ye shall bind on earth shall be bound in heaven: and whatsoever ye shall loose on earth shall be loosed in heaven. Matthew 18:17-18

These statements by Jesus are seldom understood in their proper context, but when we look at various examples of church discipline in the New Testament, we can come to a more clear understanding of what happened to Ananias and Sapphira.

In the name of our Lord Jesus Christ, when ye are gathered together, and my spirit, with the power of our Lord Jesus Christ, <u>to deliver such an one unto Satan</u> for the destruction of the flesh, that the spirit may be saved in the day of the Lord Jesus. 1 Corinthians 5:4-5

Paul used his authority for the purpose of discipline in the church.

"Know ye not that a little leaven leaveneth the whole lump? Purge out therefore the old leaven . . ." 1 Corinthians 5:6-7

*Holding faith, and a good conscience; which
some having put away concerning faith have
made shipwreck: Of whom is Hymenaeus and
Alexander; whom I have delivered unto Satan,
that they may learn not to blaspheme. 1Timothy
1:19-20*

Hymenaeus and Alexander, once in the faith had
left the faith and had begun to blaspheme. Paul being
aware of his divine authority to remit and retain sin
and to bind and loose, used this authority to purge
the church.

I believe that a case can be made for Peter having
done the same with Ananias and Sapphira. Peter
chose to retain their sin and to bind them once for
all, an act that purged the church and made certain
that those who continued to join themselves to the
Lord were of a pure heart.

*And great fear came upon all the church, and
upon as many as heard these thing. Acts 5:11*

*And of the rest durst no man join himself to
them: but the people magnified them. And
believers were the more added to the Lord,
multitudes both of men and women. Acts 13-14*

Question 25

IS CAPITAL PUNISHMENT UNGODLY?

God was the first to institute a punishment of death in the Garden of Eden. Adam and Eve were warned that if they sinned, they would die. Spiritual separation happened immediately and their physical death followed after. This "death penalty" was for the human race and established a limit or boundary to sin. Can you imagine a world in which sinful men would never die? Sin had to have a limit and God established death as its limit.

The Holy Spirit inspired Paul to write of the authority and responsibility of civil government in Romans 13. Civil government's purpose is to be a minister of God for good (Romans 13:4), and if we do evil the government does not "bear the sword in vain." This certainly refers to the government's right or duty to punish wrong doers, even to the point of wielding the sword. The government is to "execute wrath upon him that doeth evil."

Paul even included himself as a potential candidate for the death penalty. He recognized the authority of civil government to execute certain offenders.

For if I be an offender, or have committed any thing worthy of death, I refuse not to die: but if there be none of these things whereof these accuse me, no man may deliver me unto them. I appeal unto Caesar. Acts 25:11

We know that not every civil government complies with God's ways and purposes. Nevertheless, it does have God's authority to punish evil doers. Under many governments that includes capital punishment. When administered justly, it serves society and establishes the limits on certain kinds of crimes.

While capital punishment may serve as a deterrent to others, this is not its primary purpose. Its primary purpose is to deter the convicted criminal from ever murdering another person. It is a punishment that can be found under the law of God in the Old Testament and also as one of the purposes of civil government outlined in Romans 13. It does not limit the grace of God in the life of the criminal and does not prohibit salvation by faith in that grace. Capital punishment places value on the life of the victim and punishes the wrong doer in order to establish a limit to their crime.

The difference between capital punishment and murder or killing is found in the reason, the motive and under what authority the death is occurring. Murder is death which has not been sanctioned by governmental authority in accordance with the Word, the will of God and the rule of law. The act of murder demands a response by the government so society is protected according to the Word and will of God.

The commandment to not kill refers to murder as differentiated from war or civil punishment for crime. Even after the commandment to not kill (murder), God Himself sent Israel to fight against its enemies and there was great death and destruction.

All may not agree, but the concept of capital punishment does have a scriptural basis.

DID GOD DO THIS TO ME?

Question 26

MUST I OBEY THE GOVERNMENT?

Let every soul be subject unto the higher powers. For there is no power but of God: the powers that be are ordained of God. Whosoever therefore resisteth the power, resisteth the ordinance of God: and they that resist shall receive to themselves damnation. For rulers are not a terror to good works, but to the evil. Wilt thou then not be afraid of the power? do that which is good, and thou shalt have praise of the same: For he is the minister of God to thee for good. But if thou do that which is evil, be afraid; for he beareth not the sword in vain: for he is the minister of God, a revenger to execute wrath upon him that doeth evil. Wherefore ye must needs be subject, not only for wrath, but also for conscience sake. For this cause pay ye tribute also: for they are God's ministers, attending continually upon this very thing. Render therefore to all their dues: tribute to whom tribute is due; custom to whom custom; fear to whom fear; honour to whom honour. Romans 13:1-7

Romans 13:1-7 explains the relationship of the believer to the civil government. Civil government has been authorized by God for the praise of well doers and the punishment of evil doers. It is to be a minister of God to the people for good. Government is also empowered to tax, to defend and to punish.

We find a similar revelation in 1 Peter 2.

Submit yourselves to every ordinance of man for the Lord's sake: whether it be to the king, as supreme; Or unto governors, as unto them that are sent by him for the punishment of evildoers, and for the praise of them that do well. 1 Peter 2:13-14

Obviously, not all civil governments fulfill this calling as ministers of God. To the degree that we can live "a quiet and peaceable life in all godliness and honesty," (1 Timothy 2:1-3) we should not "resist the power" (Romans 13:2) and we should "do that which is good" (Romans 13:3). That would include obeying the laws of the land. When those laws force ungodly behavior on the citizens, then decisions must be made as to what extent such laws can be obeyed.

It is important to understand that it is the _concept_ of government that has been established by God, <u>not each and every kind of government nor every ruler</u>. Government has a God ordained purpose, but not every government and every leader are from God. God does not raise up ungodly governments. God's desire is that government be a tool for good and not evil.

SHOULD CHRISTIANS CELEBRATE CHRISTMAS?

It is clear that the celebration of Jesus' birth has no precedent in scripture, nor is December 25th, the day of His birth. But rather than becoming antagonistic toward Christmas, we can choose to use this opportunity to preach Jesus to those who might be more sensitive or open to the things of God due to this holiday. Christmas is what we make it, not what others considered December 25th to be many years ago. We should not let the past contaminate the present.

Many Christian families celebrate Christmas with gift giving. The Christmas tree is a seasonal decoration. Symbolic meaning can be attributed to it by some or it can simply remain a decoration that brings joy to those who see it.

Jesus knows the difference between a person putting up a Christmas tree, spending time with family and giving gifts all in love, as opposed to a pagan holiday of old where someone may have actually worshipped a tree.

Christmas should be seen as an opportunity to share with family and friends the life-changing love of God, the sending of His Son, Jesus and a way of blessing others. Some, for conscience sake, choose to not celebrate the day.

> *One man esteemeth one day above another: another esteemeth every day alike. Let every man be fully persuaded in his own mind.*
> *Romans 14:5*

The scriptures give us liberty to esteem certain days according to our own choice and desire. Many fine Christians choose to not celebrate Christmas, while others do esteem the day. Let us not judge, since it is a matter of conscience. We should be willing to rejoice with those who rejoice.

There are certainly many negative commercial aspects of the holiday, but we can look beyond that and enjoy the season giving thanks for the birth of our Lord and Savior and the tremendous act of faith it was on the part of God to love us in such a way.

Be encouraged to enjoy the Christmas season with your family and friends, giving thanks to God for His incomparable Gift.

WERE OTHER HUMANS ON THE EARTH APART FROM ADAM AND EVE?

Where did Cain's wife come from?

The Bible states that all humans have come from Adam and Eve. Eve is called the mother of all the living.

And Adam called his wife's name Eve; because she was the mother of all living. Genesis 3:20

God's mandate to Adam and Eve was that they would be fruitful and multiply and fill the earth. Obviously this meant their offspring would marry one another.

And the days of Adam after he had begotten Seth were eight hundred years: and <u>he begat sons and daughters</u>: Genesis 5:4

While Cain and Abel were the first two of Adam and Eve's children, there were no doubt many more children and descendants around at the time. We have no idea how old Cain was when he slew Abel. There may have been several generations of offspring already thriving on the earth. This seems apparent since he went off and started a city. (Genesis 4:17)

Cain married a relative as God had intended from the beginning. Later, Abraham married a half-sister. However, once God established the law in the time of Moses, such inter-family marriage was no longer permitted. We assume God made the law due to the impact of sin upon humanity, but in the beginning the effects of sin had not yet created the genetic distortions that we now see today.

Adam and Eve were created by God and were the only two humans from which the human race has come.

FINAL THOUGHTS

Without a doubt there are many more questions that merit our attention. The questions in this book are some of the most common, but I know of many others that are just as interesting. It would be good to remember that we "know in part" (1 Corinthians 13:9). We will not have all of our answers until we are with the Lord.

Beloved, now are we the sons of God, and it doth not yet appear what we shall be: but we know that, when he shall appear, we shall be like him; for we shall see him as he is. 1 John 3:2

Our confidence is in our knowledge of the nature of God. Even in the areas where we still "see through a glass darkly" (1 Corinthians 13:12), we can rest in the assurance of our righteous and loving Father who will bring all things to light.

Therefore judge nothing before the time, until the Lord come, who both will bring to light the hidden things of darkness, and will make manifest the counsels of the hearts: and then shall every man have praise of God. 1 Corinthians 4:5